BOTANICAL SANCTUARIES

Mississippi Ecoregions

- ☐ Mississippi Valley Loess Plains
- ▨ Mississippi Alluvial Plain
- ■ Southern Coastal Plain
- ☐ Southeastern Plains

1. Wall Doxey State Park
2. Great River Road State Park
3. Winterville Mounds State Park
4. Washington County Courthouse Arboretum
5. Yazoo National Wildlife Refuge (NWR)
6. Simmons Arboretum
7. Mynelle Gardens
8. Mississippi Agriculture & Forestry Museum
9. Jackson State University Botanical Garden
10. Natchez State Park
11. St. Catherine Creek NWR
12. Percy Quin State Park
13. Crosby Arboretum
14. Beauvoir, Jefferson Davis Home Botanical Gardens
15. Mississippi Sandhill Crane NWR
16. Shepard State Park
17. Paul B. Johnson State Park
18. Clarkco State Park
19. Legion State Park
20. Noxubee National Wildlife Refuge
21. Trace State Park
22. Mississippi Museum of Natural Science

Measurements denote the height of plants unless otherwise indicated. Illustrations are not to scale.

N.B. – Many edible wild plants have poisonous mimics. Never eat a wild plant or fruit unless you are absolutely sure it is safe to do so. The publisher makes no representation or warranties with respect to the accuracy, completeness, correctness or usefulness of this information and specifically disclaims any implied warranties of fitness for a particular purpose. The advice, strategies and/or techniques contained herein may not be suitable for all individuals. The publisher shall not be responsible for any physical harm (up to and including death), loss of profit or other commercial damage, the publisher assumes no liability brought or instituted by individuals or organizations arising out of or relating in any way to the application and/or use of the information, advice and strategies contained herein.

Waterford Press produces reference guides that introduce novices to nature, science, travel and languages. Product information is featured on the website: www.waterfordpress.com

Text and illustrations © 2009, 2017 by Waterford Press Inc. All rights reserved. Cover images © Shutterstock. Ecoregion map © The National Atlas of the United States. To order, call 800-434-2555. For permissions, or to share comments, e-mail editor@waterfordpress.com For information on custom-published products, call 800-434-2555 or e-mail info@waterfordpress.com

---

MISSISSIPPI TREES & WILDFLOWERS

A Folding Pocket Guide to Familiar Plants

MISSISSIPPI TREES & WILDFLOWERS – A Folding Pocket Guide to Familiar Plants

Kavanagh/Leung

TREES & SHRUBS

Longleaf Pine
Pinus palustris To 100 ft. (30 m)
Needles are up to 18 in. (45 cm) long and bundled in 3s at the ends of branchlets. Cones are cylindrical.

Spruce Pine
Pinus glabra To 100 ft. (30 m)
Needles are about 3 in. (8 cm) long and bundled in 2s. Rounded cones have scales tipped with a single prickle.

Baldcypress
Taxodium distichum To 120 ft. (36.5 m)
Note flaring trunk. Leaves are flattened and feathery. Protruding root 'knees' help to stabilize the tree in wet areas.

Black Willow
Salix nigra To 100 ft. (30 m)
Tree or shrub, often leaning. Slender leaves are shiny green on the upper surface. Flowers bloom in long, fuzzy clusters.

Eastern Cottonwood
Populus deltoides To 100 ft. (30 m)
Leaves are up to 7 in. (18 cm) long. Flowers are succeeded by capsules containing seeds with cottony 'tails'.

River Birch
Betula nigra To 80 ft. (24 m)
Has shaggy, peeling red-brown bark. Fruits are composed of winged seeds.

American Hornbeam
Carpinus caroliniana To 30 ft. (9 m)
Also called blue beech, it has blue-gray bark and a 'muscular' trunk. Distinctive fruits have seeds contained in 3-sided bracts.

White Oak
Quercus alba To 100 ft. (30 m)
Leaves have 5-9 rounded lobes. Acorn has a shallow, scaly cup.

Swamp Chestnut Oak
Quercus prinus To 80 ft. (24 m)
Leaves are up to 8 in. (20 cm) long and have toothed edges.

Basket Oak
Quercus michauxii To 130 ft. (40 m)
Bottomland species has leaves with rounded teeth. Acorns are produced in clusters of 2-3.

Willow Oak
Quercus phellos To 80 ft. (24 m)
Easily distinguished from other oaks by its narrow toothless leaves.

Water Oak
Quercus nigra To 100 ft. (30 m)
Wedge-shaped leaves are widest near the tip and up to 5 in. (13 cm) long.

TREES & SHRUBS

American Elm
Ulmus americana To 100 ft. (30 m)
Note vase-shaped profile. Leaves are toothed. Fruits have a papery collar and are notched at the tip.

Winged Elm
Ulmus alata To 80 ft. (24 m)
Saw-toothed leaves are hairy below. Twigs often have thin, 'corky' wings. Flattened fruits are hairy.

Yellow Poplar (Tuliptree)
Liriodendron tulipifera To 120 ft. (36.5 m)
Note unusual leaf shape. Showy flowers are succeeded by cone-like aggregates of papery, winged seeds.

American Beech
Fagus grandifolia To 80 ft. (24 m)
Flowers bloom in rounded clusters in spring and are succeeded by 3-sided nuts.

Sweetbay
Magnolia virginiana To 60 ft. (18 m)
Shiny, papery leaves are blunt-tipped. Cup-shaped flowers are fragrant.

Southern Magnolia
Magnolia grandiflora To 80 ft. (24 m)
Large creamy flowers, to 8 in. (20 cm) in diameter, have 9-14 petals. Cone-like, hairy fruits have bright red seeds.
State tree of Mississippi.
Blossom is the state flower.

Sweetgum
Liquidambar styraciflua To 100 ft. (30 m)
Small, greenish flowers bloom in tight, round clusters and are succeeded by hard fruits covered with woody spines.

American Sycamore
Platanus occidentalis To 100 ft. (30 m)
Leaves have 3-5 shallow lobes. Rounded fruits are bristly.

Black Cherry
Prunus serotina To 80 ft. (24 m)
Aromatic bark and leaves smell cherry-like. Dark berries have an oval stone inside.

Hawthorn
Crataegus spp. To 40 ft. (12 m)
Tree has rounded crown of spiny branches. Apple-like fruits appear in summer.

Chickasaw Plum
Prunus angustifolia To 25 ft. (7.6 m)
Thicket-forming shrub has small white flowers succeeded by edible plums.

Southern Crabapple
Malus angustifolia To 30 ft. (9 m)
Thicket-forming shrub or small tree. Fragrant pinkish flowers are succeeded by apples 1 in. (3 cm) in diameter.

TREES & SHRUBS

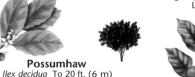

Pignut Hickory
Carya glabra To 80 ft. (24 m)
Toothed leaves have 5-7 leaflets. Flowers are succeeded by nut-like fruits.

Shagbark Hickory
Carya ovata To 100 ft. (30 m)
Bark curls away from the trunk, giving it a shaggy appearance. Leaves have 5 leaflets.

Possumhaw
Ilex decidua To 20 ft. (6 m)
Shrub or small tree has egg-shaped leaves. Bright red berries appear in the fall and persist thoughout the winter.

Common Persimmon
Diospyros virginiana To 70 ft. (21 m)
Shrub or tree has urn-shaped flowers that are succeeded by round fruits.

Yaupon
Ilex vomitoria To 20 ft. (6 m)
Alternate, evergreen leaves have wavy-toothed edges. Red, berry-like fruits persist into winter.

American Holly
Ilex opaca To 70 ft. (21 m)
Tree or shrub is distinguished by its stiff, spiny evergreen leaves and red, poisonous berries.

Boxelder
Acer negundo To 60 ft. (18 m)
Leaves have 3-7 leaflets. Seeds are encased in paired papery keys.

Silver Maple
Acer saccharinum To 80 ft. (24 m)
Note short trunk and spreading crown. 5-lobed leaves are silvery beneath.

Red Maple
Acer rubrum To 90 ft. (27 m)
Leaves have 3-5 lobes and turn scarlet in autumn. Flowers are succeeded by red, winged seed pairs.

Black Tupelo
Nyssa sylvatica To 100 ft. (30 m)
Glossy leaves turn red in autumn. Blue fruits have ridged seeds.

Flowering Dogwood
Cornus florida To 30 ft. (9 m)
Tiny yellow flowers bloom in crowded clusters surrounded by 4 white petal-like structures.

Black Walnut
Juglans nigra To 90 ft. (27 m)
Leaves have 9-23 leaflets. Greenish fruits have a black nut inside.

TREES & SHRUBS

Green Ash
Fraxinus pennsylvanica To 60 ft. (18 m)
Leaves have 7-9 leaflets. Flowers are succeeded by single-winged fruits.

Sugarberry
Celtis laevigata To 80 ft. (24 m)
Bark is covered with 'corky' warts. Fleshy fruits contain a single seed.

Sassafras
Sassafras albidum To 60 ft. (18 m)
Aromatic tree or shrub has leaves that are mitten-shaped or 3-lobed. Fruits are dark berries.

Red Buckeye
Aesculus pavia To 20 ft. (6 m)
Tree or shrub grows in moist soils. Leaves have 5-7 leaflets. Nut-like fruits contain 1-2 poisonous seeds.

Spicebush
Lindera benzoin To 17 ft. (5.1 m)
Shrub has small yellow flowers succeeded by bright red berries.

Southern Bayberry
Myrica cerifera To 30 ft. (9 m)
Common on wet and well-drained soils. Fruits have a waxy coating and were once used to make candles.

Southern Catalpa
Catalpa bignonioides To 50 ft. (15 m)
Tree has heart-shaped leaves, large clusters of flowers and a bean-like fruit.

Witch Hazel
Hamamelis virginiana To 30 ft. (9 m)
Shrub or small tree. Tiny yellow flowers bloom along leafless twigs in the fall. Woody fruits eject their seeds when ripe.

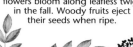

Common Serviceberry
Amelanchier arborea To 50 ft. (15 m)
White, star-shaped flowers are succeeded by red to purple-black berries.

Winged Sumac
Rhus copallina To 18 ft. (5.4 m)
Flowers bloom in dense upright clusters and are succeeded by berry-like fruits.

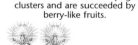

Kudzu
Pueraria montana Vine to 75 ft. (23 m)
Introduced species often over-runs buildings and fencerows.

Buttonbush
Cephalanthus occidentalis To 10 ft. (3 m)
'Pincushion' flowers have protruding stamens.

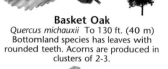

Bloodroot
Sanguinaria canadensis
To 10 in. (25 cm)
Root has a reddish sap.

Fragrant Water Lily
Nymphaea odorata
Flower to 6 in.
(15 cm) wide.

Mayapple
Podophyllum peltatum
To 18 in. (45 cm)
Cup-shaped flowers
bloom between 2
leaves. Fruits are yellow.

Daisy Fleabane
Erigeron annuus
To 5 ft. (1.5 m)
Flowers are white
to pinkish or purple.

Calico Aster
*Symphyotrichum
lateriflorium*
To 5 ft. (150 cm)

Lizard Tail
*Saururus
cernuus*
To 5 ft.
(1.5 m)

Oxeye Daisy
Leucanthemum vulgare
To 3 ft. (90 cm)
Showy flowers bloom
along roadsides
in summer.

Horsenettle
Solanum carolinense
To 3 ft. (90 cm)
Note broad-toothed
leaves and spiny stems.
Flowers are white to pink.

White Sweet Clover
Melilotus alba
To 8 ft. (2.4 m)
Leafy plant has long
spikes of tiny, white
pea-shaped flowers.

Boneset
Eupatorium perfoliatum
To 4 ft. (1.2 m)
Hairy plant with stout,
erect stem. Fuzzy,
white flowers bloom
in dense clusters.

Shooting Star
Dodecatheon meadia
To 2 ft. (60 cm)

Solomon's Zigzag
*Maianthemum
racemosum*
To 3 ft. (90 cm)
Note kinked stem.

Yarrow
*Achillea
millefolium*
To 3 ft. (90 cm)
Leaves are
fern-like.

Arrowhead
Sagittaria spp.
To 4 ft. (1.2 m)
Aquatic plant has
arrow-shaped
leaves.

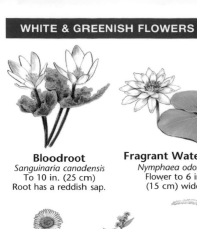

Queen Anne's Lace
Daucus spp.
To 4 ft. (1.2 m)
Flower clusters
become cup-
shaped as
they age.

Pussytoes
Antennaria spp.
To 16 in. (40 cm)
Woolly stalks
support fluffy
flowerheads.

Indian Pipe
*Monotropa
uniflora*
To 10 in. (25 cm)
Waxy white plant
is parasitic on
other plants
in shady woods.

Nodding Ladys' Tresses
Spiranthes cernua
To 2 ft. (60 cm)
Flowers bloom in
spiral rows on
flower stalk.

Multiflora Rose
Rosa multiflora
To 15 ft. (4.5 m)
Bushy shrub is an
aggressive invasive plant.

Jack-in-the-Pulpit
Arisaema triphyllum
To 3 ft. (90 cm)
Club-like stem is
surrounded by a
curving, green
to purplish hood.

Jimson Weed
Datura stramonium
To 5 ft. (1.5 m)

Shrubby Cinquefoil
Potentilla simplex
Stems to 3 ft. (90 cm)
Sprawling roadside
plant has leaves
with 5 leaflets.

Yellow Jessamine
Gelsemium sempervirens
Vine to 17 ft.
(5.1 m) long

Black-eyed Susan
Rudbeckia hirta
To 3 ft. (90 cm)
Flower has a dark,
conical central disk.

Evening Primrose
Oenothera biennis
To 5 ft. (1.5 m)
Lemon-scented,
4-petalled flowers
bloom in the evening.

Golden Coreopsis
Coreopsis tinctoria
To 4 ft. (1.2 m)
Flower rays have
brown bases.

Yellow Trumpets
Sarracenia alata
To 2 ft. (60 cm)
Carnivorous plant has
pitcher-shaped leaves
that trap insects.

Hawkweed
Hieracium spp.
To 2 ft. (60 cm)
Hairy plant has leaves
clustered at its base.

Compass Plant
Silphium laciniatum
To 12 ft. (3.6 m)
The plant's leaves
tend to orient in a
north-south direction.

Common Mullein
Verbascum thapsus
To 7 ft. (2.1 m)
Common
roadside weed.

Goldenrod
*Solidago
gigantea*
To 6.5 ft.
(2 m)

Butterfly Weed
Asclepias tuberosa
To 3 ft. (90 cm)
Orange flowers
are star-shaped.

Yellow Lady's Slipper
*Cypripedium
parviflorum*
To 22 in. (55 cm)

Day Lily
Hemerocallis fulva
To 4 ft. (1.2 m)

Cross Vine
Bignonia capreolata
Vine to 20 ft. (6 m)

Jewelweed
Impatiens spp.
To 5 ft. (1.5 m)
Spotted, orange-yellow
flowers are horn-shaped.
Ripe seed capsules
burst when touched.

Indian Strawberry
Duchesnea indica
To 3 in. (7.5 cm)

Seedbox
*Ludwigia
alternifolia*
To 3 in. (7.5 cm)

Partridge Pea
Cassia fasciculata
To 30 in. (75 cm)
Leaves have 6-18
pairs of leaflets.

Prickly Pear
Opuntia humifusa
To 12 in. (30 cm)
Clumps to 3 ft.
(90 cm) wide.

Pineweed
*Hypericum
gentianoides*
To 20 in. (50 cm)

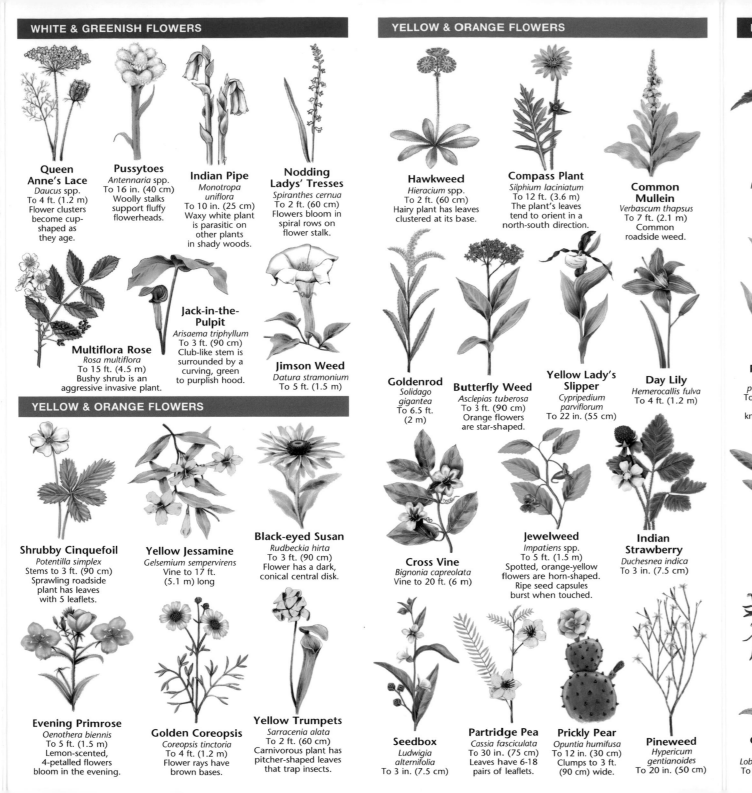

Swamp Rose Mallow
Hibiscus grandiflorus
To 36 in. (90 cm)

Wild Geranium
Geranium maculatum
To 2 ft. (60 cm)

Common Morning Glory
Ipomoea purpurea
Stems to 10 ft. (3 m) long.
Creeping plant.

Pinkweed
*Polygonum
pensylvanicum*
To 4 ft. (1.2 m)
Stems have
knot-like joints.

Handsome Blazing Star
Liatris aspera
To 4 ft. (1.2 m)

Smooth Phlox
Phlox glaberrima
To 20 in. (50 cm)

Common Milkweed
Asclepias syriaca
To 6 ft. (1.8 m)
Pink-purple flowers
bloom in drooping
clusters.

Wild Azalea
*Rhododendron
canescens*
To 15 ft. (4.5 m)

Sensitive Brier
Mimosa microphylla
To 18 in. (45 cm)
Vine-like herb.

Coral Honeysuckle
Lonicera sempervirens
Vine to 17 ft. (5.1 m)

Cardinal Flower
Lobelia cardinalis
To 4 ft. (1.2 m)

Showy Evening Primrose
Oenothera speciosa
To 2 ft. (60 cm)
Flowers bloom in
the evening.

Fire Pink
Silene virginica
To 2 ft. (60 cm)

Indian Pink
Spigelia marilandica
To 2 ft. (60 cm)

Cypressvine
Ipomoea quamoclit
Climbing to
9 ft. (270 cm)

Trumpet Creeper
Campsis radicans
Vine to 20 ft. (6 m)
A hummingbird
favorite.

Crimson Pitcher Plant
*Sarracenia
leucophylla*
To 36 in. (90 cm)

Little Sweet Betsy
Trillium cuneatum
To 18 in. (45 cm)

Red Turtlehead
Chelone oblique
To 36 in. (90 cm)
Flowers resemble
turtle heads.

Spring Beauty
Claytonia virginica
To 12 in. (30 cm)

Bull Thistle
Cirsium vulgare
To 6 ft. (1.8 m)

Red Clover
Tritolium pratense
To 2 ft. (60 cm)
Leaves have
3 leaflets.

Bluets
Houstonia spp.
To 6 in. (15 cm)
Yellow-centered flowers
grow in large colonies.

Blue-eyed Grass
*Sisyrinchium
angustifolium*
To 20 in. (50 cm)

Eastern Blue Curls
Trichostema spp.
To 30 in. (75 cm)

Iris
Iris spp.
To 3 ft.
(90 cm)

Wild Petunia
Ruellia humilis
To 32 in. (80 cm)
Trumpet-shaped flowers
close in the evening.

Passionflower
Passiflora incarnata
Climbing vine
to 20 ft. (6 m) high.
Flowers have a fringe
of 'tentacles'.

Giant Ironweed
Vernonia gigantea
To 8 ft. (2.4 m)

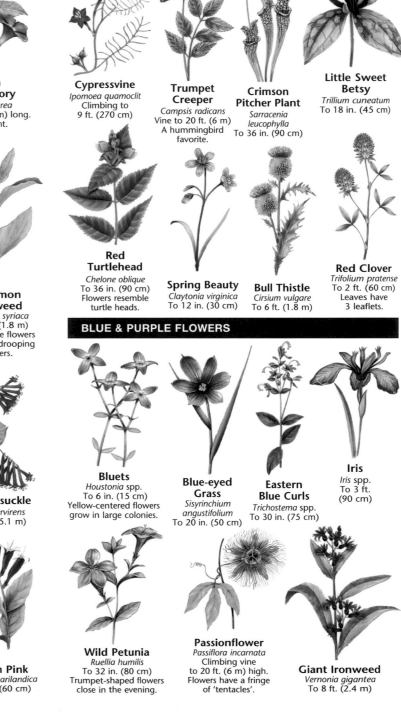

Purple Coneflower
Echinacea spp.
To 5 ft. (1.5 m)

Hairy Skullcap
Scutellaria elliptica
To 30 in. (75 cm)

Carolina Vetch
Vicia caroliniana
To 30 in. (75 cm)

Beardtongue
Penstemon spp.
To 18 in. (45 cm)

Downy Lobelia
Lobelia puberula
To 5 ft. (1.5 m)

Jacob's Ladder
Polemonium reptans
To 18 in. (45 cm)
Leaves have
rung-like leaflets.

Dayflower
Commelina spp.
To 3 ft. (90 cm)
Flowers have two
large blue petals
above a tiny
white one.

Wild Blue Phlox
Phlox divaricata
To 20 in. (50 cm)

Round-lobed Hepatica
Hepatica nobilis
To 6 in. (15 cm)

Virginia Bluebells
Mertensia virginica
To 2 ft. (60 cm)

Wisteria
Wisteria frutescens
Vine to 50 ft. (15 m)
Grows in thickets.

Great Blue Lobelia
Lobelia siphilitica
To 4 ft. (1.2 m)

Common Blue Violet
Viola spp.
To 8 in. (20 cm)

Heal-all
Prunella vulgaris
To 12 in. (30 cm)
Flowers have a
fringed lower lip.

Spiderwort
Tradescantia spp.
To 3 ft. (90 cm)

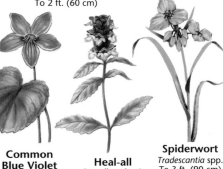